Understanding Coding with

HOPSCOTCH

Patricia Harris

PowerKiDS
press

New York

Published in 2016 by The Rosen Publishing Group, Inc.
29 East 21st Street, New York, NY 10010

First Edition

Editor: Greg Roza
Book Design: Michael J. Flynn

Photo Credits: Cover Stephen Simpson/Iconica/Getty Images; cover, pp. 3–24 (coding background) Lukas Rs/Shutterstock.com; p. 5 karelnoppe/Shutterstock.com; p. 7 Martin Barraud/Caiaimage/Getty Images; p. 9 Pressmaster/Shutterstock.com; pp. 11–12, 14–17, 19 (Hopscotch imagery) courtesy of Hopscotch Technologies, Inc.; p. 13 Samuel Borges/Shutterstock.com; p. 20 Golden Pixels LLC/Shutterstock.com; p. 21 cowardlion/Shutterstock.com.

Cataloging-in-Publication Data

Harris, Patricia.
Understanding coding with hopscotch / by Patricia Harris.
p. cm. — (Kids can code)
Includes index.
ISBN 978-1-5081-4459-5 (pbk.)
ISBN 978-1-4994-1861-3 (6-pack)
ISBN 978-1-5081-4460-1 (library binding)
1. Computer programming — Juvenile literature. 2. Programming languages (Electronic computers) — Juvenile literature. I. Harris, Patricia, 1949-. II. Title.
QA76.52 H37 2016
005.1—d23

Manufactured in the United States of America

CPSIA Compliance Information: Batch #BW16PK: For Further Information contact Rosen Publishing, New York, New York at 1-800-237-9932

Contents

Playgrounds and Computers............4

Scratch.............................6

Play by the Rules...................8

Getting Started....................10

Drag and Drop......................12

My Abilities.......................14

Background.........................16

Play with Hopscotch................18

Get Hopping!.......................20

Blocks in Hopscotch................22

Glossary...........................23

Index..............................24

Websites...........................24

Playgrounds and Computers

Have you ever played the playground game hopscotch? Players first draw a group of connected blocks and label them with numbers. Then, they take turns hopping from one box to the next. It's a fun game that almost anyone can play and enjoy.

The **computer language** called Hopscotch has something in common with the playground game of the same name. It features colorful blocks for coding instead of lines of text. This allows users to drag and drop coding instructions from a list to a work space on the computer screen. When put together, these blocks create moving images on the screen. Coders of all ages can create **animations**, games, stories, and more. Hopscotch allows new coders to see results in very little time.

Breaking the Code

Not all programming languages use blocks and images like Hopscotch does. Most languages use lines of text called code.

Hopscotch is a program for use on iPads and iPhones. The team that made the program hopes to expand to other **platforms** in the future.

Scratch

Hopscotch was based on a similar programming language called Scratch. Both are free online apps, or applications, and both feature colorful blocks that users drag and drop to create **scripts**. The team that made Hopscotch wanted to make a version of Scratch that was even easier to use. They removed some kinds of blocks found in Scratch and added some new ones.

Coding was once considered an activity for scientists and geniuses. However, programming languages such as Scratch and Hopscotch have proven that anyone can code. They teach new coders, young and old, the basics of programming and prepare them for more advanced languages. The groups of blocks show users how to group **commands** while coding. Most important, Hopscotch makes coding fun!

Breaking the Code

Software that's free for anyone to use, such as Hopscotch, is called open-source software.

If you want to experiment with Hopscotch, you need to **download** it first. Ask your parents to help you install it on your iPad or iPhone.

Play by the Rules

Before you can begin to learn about coding in any language, Hopscotch included, you need to know that computer programming is about following rules. That may sound a little like playing a game with rules, and it can be just as fun.

Rule 1: Coders must know what they want the computer to do and write a plan.

Rule 2: Coders must use special words to have the computer take **input**, make choices, and take action.

Rule 3: Coders need to think about what tasks can be put into a group.

Rule 4: Coders need to employ **logic** using AND, OR, NOT, and other logic statements as key words.

Rule 5: Coders must explore the **environment** and understand how it works.

Breaking the Code

The environment for Hopscotch is a GUI (GOO-ee), or graphical user Interface. The GUI environment makes programming easier.

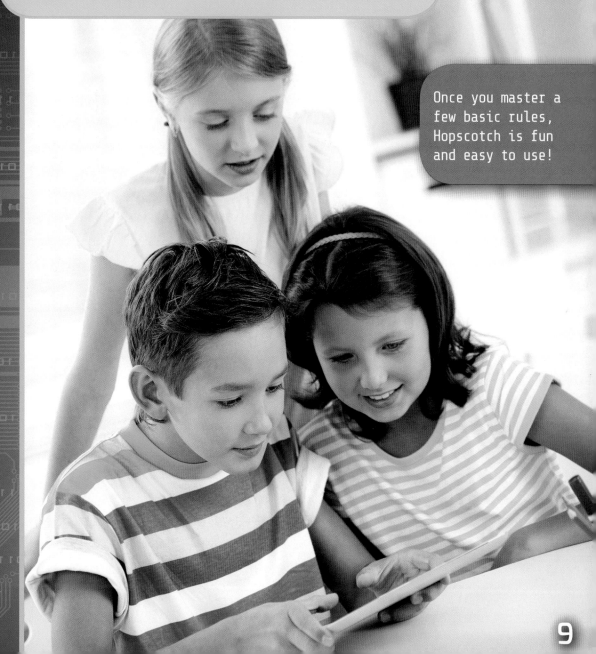

Once you master a few basic rules, Hopscotch is fun and easy to use!

9

Getting Started

Hopscotch is a program used to create animations, games, and more. You create your own backgrounds, choose characters that can move around the screen, and add sounds. When you first download the program, it comes with some simple games to help you learn a little more about Hopscotch. The games are under the choice called "levels." They're fun and help you understand some concepts you need for programming.

You choose a character that programmers sometimes call a sprite. By dragging new blocks into the work space, you can give the sprite abilities. Then, just keep adding different code to add more to your animation. You can add a background by using Drawing Blocks to create lines in different places on the screen in different colors, widths, and directions.

Breaking the Code

Before you begin, you must have a plan. You must think about input, choices, and actions. You must think about grouping commands and being logical.

CHARACTERS

BACKGROUND

Coders plan first, but sometimes have to "play" with the code to get the results they want.

Drag and Drop

Before you begin to work, you must understand the Hopscotch GUI. Here's a picture of the screen for Hopscotch. On the left is the box where you select actions. The dropdown arrows let you see the actions in each section. Sometimes you may see the word "more," and more options will be shown when you click it.

This is a small part of a program to draw a background. You can see the blocks of code and how some of them are grouped together within purple Drawing Blocks.

On the right is the work area where you drag and drop the blocks. You can click the "Show Preview" button on the left to play a small version of the program or the "Play" button to see a full-screen version. You can try out actions one at a time by dragging the action to the right, clicking the "Play" button, and then dragging the action back to the left to delete it.

My Abilities

Writing the code to make a character move is easy. First, you need to think about what you want to do. Your plan could be: I want a monkey to run across my screen a little way, then spin around and grow bigger. All you would need to do is choose your character and the actions you want from the My Abilities box. Below is the code for this plan.

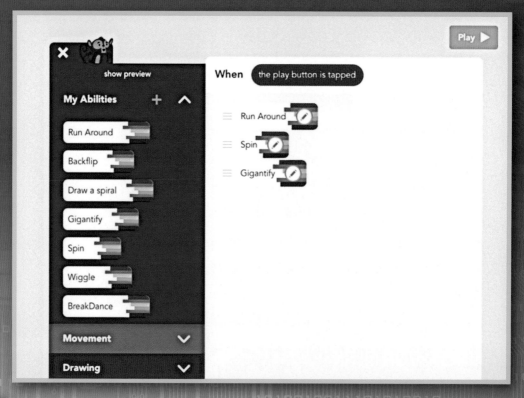

The My Abilities actions let you start writing a program right away. The pencil after each ability shows you the commands that make up that ability. The code for "Run Around" is shown to the right. Notice that this ability uses code that's grouped. It starts with the ability at the beginning and the word "end" when the code is finished for this ability.

The green "Change Pose" block makes the picture of the monkey change so it looks like the character is changing direction.

Background

Next, you can add a background to your plan: I want the monkey to cross a screen with a background that has a tree, grass, and sky.

Making a background means you will write your own **loop**. Then, you will place the tree where you want it. You go to a blank plan and choose the tree character. At "add a new rule," drag over "the play button is tapped." Drag the blocks in order as shown on the code at right.

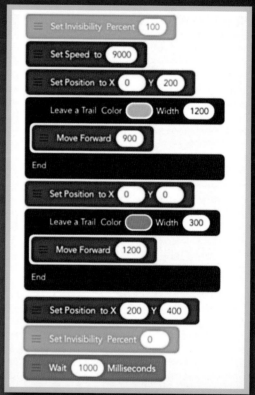

After playing your code to be sure the background works, press the "Edit" button. Click on the + and choose the monkey. When you press "Play," your grass and sky will appear, and the monkey will run across the screen. This matches the original plan.

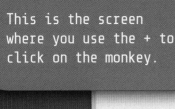

This is the screen where you use the + to click on the monkey.

When the play button is tapped
Set Invisibility…

+ Add a new rule

Banyan

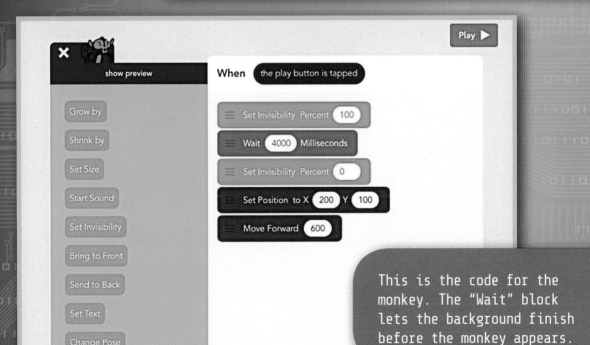

show preview

Grow by

Shrink by

Set Size

Start Sound

Set Invisibility

Bring to Front

Send to Back

Set Text

Change Pose

Play ▶

When   the play button is tapped

Set Invisibility Percent 100

Wait 4000 Milliseconds

Set Invisibility Percent 0

Set Position to X 200 Y 100

Move Forward 600

This is the code for the monkey. The "Wait" block lets the background finish before the monkey appears.

Play with Hopscotch

When you want to create your own animation, here are the steps to follow:

1. **Write out a simple plan.**
   I want a character to dance across a scene.

2. **Choose your character and design your background.**
   I want a monkey in a field.

3. **Think about actions you can group together as a repeat.**
   I want the monkey to spin five times.

4. **Think about any logic you would need to use.**
   I want my monkey to walk AND spin AND flip.

5. **Code.**

Now you're ready to try out the code and change it any way you like! You can download the app for Hopscotch on a tablet for free. Setting up an account lets you share your work.

Here is code that makes your field and sky.

When the play button is tapped — To start the program.

Set Invisibility Percent 100 — Hides the character and speeds up the process.

Set Speed to 9000

Set Position to X 50 Y 50 — Sets the starting place in bottom left corner.

Leave a Trail Color Width 400

Move Forward 900 — A special routine to draw the grass.

End

Set Position to X 50 Y 500 — Sets the starting place in top left corner.

Leave a Trail Color Width 600

Move Forward 900 — A special routine to draw the sky.

End

Here is some code you add to make the monkey dance.

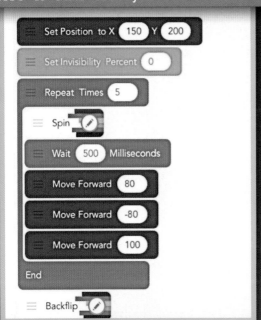

Set Position to X 150 Y 200 — Sets the starting place on the grass.

Set Invisibility Percent 0 — Shows the drawing shape.

Repeat Times 5 — Starts a loop to repeat the dance 5 times.

Spin

Wait 500 Milliseconds — The dance is a spin and a forward and backward movement.

Move Forward 80

Move Forward -80 — Backward movement is forward with a minus sign!

Move Forward 100

End — Ends the loop.

Backflip — Ends dance with a backflip.

19

Get Hopping!

Do you want to become a coder? There are countless projects for coders to experiment with using Hopscotch. One of the greatest things about using Hopscotch is sharing your creations with other coders who enjoy using the colorful coding program. However, the sharing part of Hopscotch is not **monitored**. The levels and activities are by the people who wrote the app. Before you go to share or download programs from other users in "Explore," check in with an adult.

Like many hobbies or jobs, learning to code takes some time and patience. However, learning to code with Hopscotch can make the process fun and easy, just like the playground game by the same name. Now it's time to get hopping!

Learning to code is easier than most people think, especially with a program like Hopscotch.

21

Blocks in Hopscotch

Control Block —A blue block that determines how often actions are repeated and how much time passes between movements.

Drawing Block —A purple block that allows users to draw lines and shade areas of the background.

Looks and Sounds Block —A green block that changes what the character looks and sounds like.

Movement Block —A red block that controls how the character moves.

My Abilities Block —A rainbow-colored block that allows users to select previously coded actions.

Glossary

animation: A movie made from a series of drawings, photographs, or computer graphics that creates the appearance of motion by small progressive changes in each image.

command: A code or message that tells a computer to do something.

computer language: A programming language designed to give instructions to a computer.

download: Copy data from one computer to another, often over the Internet.

environment: The combination of computer hardware and software that allows a user to perform various tasks.

input: Information that is entered into a computer.

logic: A proper or reasonable way of thinking about or understanding something.

loop: A process the starts over once it reaches the end.

monitor: To observe and check the progress of something.

platform: The programs and equipment that make up a particular computer and determine how it works.

script: A sequence of instructions carried out by a computer program.

Index

A

abilities, 10, 15
action, 8, 10, 12, 13,
     14, 15, 18, 22
animations, 4, 10, 18

B

backgrounds, 10, 12,
     16, 17, 18, 22
blocks, 4, 6, 10, 12, 13,
     15, 16, 17, 22

C

characters, 10, 11, 14,
     15, 16, 18, 19, 22
choices, 8, 10
commands, 6, 10, 15
Control Block, 22

D

drag and drop, 4, 6, 10,
     13, 16
Drawing Blocks, 10, 12,
     22

E

environment, 8, 9

G

games, 4, 8, 10
GUI, 9, 12

I

input, 8, 10

L

logic, 8, 10, 18
Looks and Sounds
     Block, 22
loop, 16, 19

M

Movement Block, 22
My Abilities, 14, 15, 22

P

plan, 8, 10, 11, 14, 16,
     18
programming language,
     4, 6, 8

R

rules, 6, 9, 16

S

Scratch, 6
scripts, 6
sprite, 10

Websites

Due to the changing nature of Internet links, PowerKids Press has developed an
online list of websites related to the subject of this book. This site is updated regularly.
Please use this link to access the list: www.powerkidslinks.com/kcc/hops